CW00871855

Reflections of Life

Richard Azael Martinez Jr.

iUniverse

REFLECTIONS OF LIFE

iUniverse books may be ordered through booksellers or by contacting:

iUniverse
1663 Liberty Drive
Bloomington, IN 47403
www.iuniverse.com
1-800-Authors (1-800-288-4677)

ISBN: 978-1-5320-9224-4 (sc)
ISBN: 978-1-5320-9231-2 (hc)
ISBN: 978-1-5320-9225-1 (e)

Library of Congress Control Number: 2020901237

Print information available on the last page.

iUniverse rev. date: 01/25/2020

Contents

Love Is a Drug

I need a quick fix.
I'm addicted to you.
Feeling high, feeling low,
What to do?
An aphrodisiac,
Affection in a sack.
I can feel you in my veins.
I'm stuck without a track.
I'm drowning in a bottle
Of absolute sorrow.
If I can't see you now,
There will be no tomorrow.
Pure euphoria.
When I'm with you, it's ecstasy.
I take so much of you in
That I can't even see.
I might have to quit cold turkey.
I might have to wean.
Love is a drug.
You already proved it to me.

Waste of Breath

Sometimes I think that
when I talk, people don't listen.
I think that because
when they respond, they say something different,
and when they say something different,
I don't understand.
It gets me frustrated and all out of hand.
It makes me feel like saying something
that will make them understand, that will make them understand,
to their face
so they can think first
and that puts them in their place.
I'm the nicest guy who can be,
so I wonder if the next time I'm having a conversation,
if that person doesn't listen,
remember just to have patience
or just stop talking,
wasting my breath,
and just try to be friends with the person.
Waiting for the next step,
but what is that step?
Some say walk away,
knowing that person
had really nothing to say.

Mother Earth

It spins, it glows.
From afar it shows
that hue of blue on
which life can grow.
The green of trees,
the land, and all its girth,
who would have dreamed up
this beautiful Mother Earth?
Wonderful features,
wonderful creatures,
wonderful creations,
and wonderful teachers,
learning, evolving,
problem-resolving,
nature's fury, and nature's calming.
There is no need to look
throughout the universe
for a place to live but right here on
beautiful Mother Earth.

Don't Be Scared

Don't be scared
To tell me what you feel
Because I know what's
Empty and what's real.
Don't be scared
To show me something new
Because what we have
Is only between me and you.
Don't be scared
To follow your dreams.
It's a road to happiness
However hard it seems.
Don't be scared
Every time we are apart
Because I'm still with you,
Right next to your heart.
Don't be scared
Of things to come.
When it's all said and done,
You're the one.

Thinking Out Loud

I see the earth.
Then I see the clouds.
I see a door.
Now I'm thinking out loud.
The planes they pass
In increments on their way
To see their tomorrow
And see a brighter day.
Birds of all kinds,
They try and follow.
The birds were the ones that showed the planes
All about tomorrow.
When there are no other sounds,
I look around
Profoundly enough.
Without a word, the world is still round.
The blue behind the clouds,
It speaks for itself.
Eyes in the world,
Seeing everyone, so it helps.
All the lost love
And the souls that want to make you cry.
So I think of the words I'm writing
And never ask why to the sky.
On the beach the water comes in.
Then the water goes out.
La Luna is half full.

Darker are the clouds.
Now the radiating love
From the earth is renowned.
Writing down what I see
Just from thinking out loud.
I think to myself,
Is peace justified by a word
Or people?
Me, I personally think,
Peace is when minds agree on love, not hate,
While having a drink.
That's priceless, no mistake.
Remaking old times
For memories' sake
From night until
The moment again we wake.
My thoughts have transcended.
Hopefully, you can hear me now.
Renowned's the word
Just from thinking out loud.

Beautiful Miss Monroe

Do you remember Miss Monroe?
She was beautiful.
She was sweet as a rose.
Why did she have to overdose?
She married DiMaggio.
She was a centerfold.
She had the world in a hold
Because her beauty flowed.
The first of her kind,
And she blew people's minds.
Maybe the first of her kind,
With looks that could stop time.
Hollywood stars
And the silver screen,
Once people saw her,
Such beauty they'd never seen.
Short-lived life
On the planet Earth,
Priceless and worthy of
Beautiful Miss Monroe.
Why did you have to go?
Now heaven's angel,
Even more beautiful.

All Used Up

Women can use men
just as men can use women.
It's been like this
from the very beginning.
Loving for money,
or maybe for control,
sometimes it's not pretty,
an ugly thing to behold.
For some it's a habit,
like smoking tobacco,
a habit so bad
it's not good for the soul.
But to be judged for something
that's not a crime
can cause animosity.
For something so benign,
and it's right in front of you,
some can't see 'cause love is blind,
and they get hurt in the end
for wasting their time.

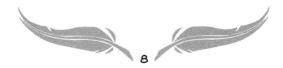

Waiting for the Sun

I can't sleep.
Waiting for tomorrow to come.
Waiting for the moon
To be replaced by the sun.
Waiting for the stars at night,
That sparkle and shine so bright,
To fade from the first light.
And the clouds of white
On a background shade of blue.
But first come different colors
Before sunrise comes through.
There's nothing to say,
There's nothing to do,
Except think about the day
That is becoming new.
But until it comes,
I will be the one
To wait with faith
And greet the sun.

Choices

The choices we make,
The choices we break,
Sometimes faking and taking.
Alone someone can stay
If we choose to lose.
Then we are set up for defeat.
Do we want an audience
For everyone to meet?
That's not really fair
To those who have been chosen,
Close to you
Or in the wide open.
So closing the door
On a caring person
Can leave you astray
And break the heart of your hopeful day.
The day is yours.
When we say these are the chances
To be who we are
And make a choice at a glance,
And at a glimpse of an eye,
Asking why,
The choice is yours.
Don't be afraid to see what it's for.
The day with family
Or your higher power,
The clouds and everything underneath,

Can make your choices a solid tower
In which no one can meet,
So there is no defeat.
A world with words
Of undoubted things,
The doubt of a choice
Can change and might just so do.
Confidence will change it
Through and through.
Don't give up.
Every day can be your day.

Tell Me Something about This Hurricane

Tell me something about this hurricane.
I almost tripped.
Living in society,
Now it's ripped.
We must recover
Like no other.
We must reunite,
Sticking together at night.
Please, no more for the deficit.
But insurance makes the wallet tight.
My vision now
Is for a positive sight.
Happens every time I pray.
In the sacred,
Goes without a doubt,
To victims of the storm where I was born
Over the ocean waters.
Fathers, mothers, sons, and daughters,
Things happened never thought of.
Businesses, salons,
And restaurants too.
Places we step into
With our blessed shoes
 Just to feel at home,

To feel your heart warm.
My heart goes out to victims of storms,
To rebuild what was sworn,
To those who have lost,
Or anything with foundation.
We've no need to worry
Because the Lord's time is never wasted.

My Piano

A finger touches the key,
Hard or soft.
Then a sound comes from the hammer
That hits the string that is taut.
One of the most beautiful sounds
A person can hear.
Who thought a wooden box could sound
So dear,
Near to the heart?
Once the sounds start
And the notes transcend
To a work of art,
Any note you pick
Can start a reaction
To another uprising of
Melodic magic.
This is similar to how I feel
About the piano that is heard.
For me an explanation,
My piano is too beautiful for words.

Homeless, Madness

The Day Saves Me

My past.
Night work clears the mind.
Contemplations, though,
Of every kind.
Wishing for a time machine
To mend broken ways.
Wind from the bay
As the moon and clouds play.
I look up and see a star,
Wondering if others I know see the same thing,
Hoping that another daybreak
Doesn't bring another broken wing.
Singing sometimes boisterous,
Sometimes melancholy, is how I feel.
The hands of time touch the people who were real.
So many, I think,
Have they loved and lost.
Happiness fulfills
When the children play in the park.
Another dollar, another day
To make my mark.

Life's Consequences

I wonder about the demeanor
That people's personalities bring,
Like when a man gives love to a woman
That makes the birds sing.
Does she really want to
Spend the rest of her life with him?
Or is her biological clock ticking,
So she goes out on a whim?
Things like that
Make me wonder a lot.
Makes me think about the minds people got.
Like a convict in jail,
Left there to rot,
Constantly thinking about
The person he shot.
Pray some more.
I hope the wrongly accused
May see the light of day.
What is there to say?
Some say locked away.
Or a young family
With no money for rent to pay,
So they're living in a shelter
With nowhere else to stay.
Their demeanor may be good,
But their hope can go astray.
They may have a strong bond,

But it can be better or worse the next day.
I take for granted
All these things I have to say,
Like clothes, food, and a home
That I take advantage of every day.
What about a baby,
Sucking on his or her thumb,
Who has an addict for a mother
And a father on the run?
Is it going to be any harder
For that baby growing up,
Not knowing his or her parents?
I would say that's pretty tough.
Why can somebody go on about hardships,
The hardships of life?
I pray to the Almighty to make things all right.

Deserving Days

Who cares about failures?
At what cost?
The ones who deserve
are not the ones who lost.
How many times
does a person have to hear
the same thing,
reminders on how a day
comes to night, and we sing?
Discriminatory people
who try to find themselves
make it through,
letting go after a period of time.
Finally finding out after years
they wasted their own lives.
With that said and everything that led,
the voices in your head
come to rest instead.

Numb

I may know of love.
I may know of faith.
Even if I did,
I'm not sure what difference it would make.
A cold heart
Because the struggle of life,
Used up and confused.
Don't know wrong from right.
Wondering if I die,
Would I really see a light?
But how can that be
If my eyes are closed tight?
The human spirit,
Most believe it's there.
But if I found mine,
Then I would care
To speak of these things
Most would not dare
Because of sin and bad karma.
But they will curse and swear.
Contradiction,
The mother of falsehoods.
Because when it happens,
You don't know if it's bad or good.
Numb is asking for help on a sidewalk.
Some would cry.
Some would watch.

The numb wouldn't even break stride.
We don't understand unless we see
The facts firsthand.
I'm possibly numb.
Most say it already because they can.

Jealousy

Jealousy breeds hate to me.
It can put a man down quickly.
An impulse from the brain,
A simple feeling, nothing tricky.
But you feel you're getting tricked.
It can change thoughts quick,
Like a fatal hit to the head
Or a stab from a pick.
It can eat a man or woman
From the inside out.
Jealousy, without a doubt,
Can make the wrong words come out.
And if that happens to be,
You could be living at that person's mercy.
And if you pretend it isn't there,
The feeling can be worse than if you can see.
One can care for another
In a different way they can't understand.
You think you're in control
But really eating out of their hand.

Found

If I leave everything behind,
Will I still be the same?
If I don't remain kind,
Is there another place to stop emotional pain?
I met so many.
I greet them with my all.
Many times fell in love.
Which angel had to fall?
Take care, good luck,
Congratulations.
Maybe intelligence to all I hear.
With the problems that I'm facing,
Everybody who cared
Left without a trace.
Still so many involved.
Don't want to show face.
Possibly a friend at a time,
Still with communication.
Hope is not lost but found
From keeping down.
Am I still found?
Am I still found?

What Do I Stand For?

By myself again,
writing with my pen,
staying humble to stomach,
who came home again,
staying the same.
Knowing things will never change
unless I take it upon myself,
all with no help.
I pray to the Lord if there were feelings felt
on land I never meant
to the sea shelf.
Thinking of an island in the ocean,
floating on transit to make a name for myself,
pretending to be somebody else.
I cannot do that, so
to my right to keeping these
thoughts alone,
prone to mental injury,
was this meant to be?
Agreed to see anybody else's thoughts
to be believed, needed, and wanted
in a place of flaunted stunts,
purity with love.
Hustling my own rights of the years and months.
Just look above.

The Pill

An Eye for an Eye

An eye for an eye.
Blocked minds.
Everything is blocked
With an order to subside.
Give up?
Blame is the game.
Some can't let go.
Who is to blame?
Blame me.
Why blame twice?
I've learned it's not a good feeling
To feel blame at night.
Love measured
By what you do.
Also not to be disrespectful to a person.
That has no prayers for you.
Is it anybody's business?
Listen to the reaction; it may be fair
In layman's terms.
Don't try to ruin
for whom you most care.

Rain in My Mind

Rain in my mind.
Thinking of a beach,
Anywhere I can relax
And soak my feet.
Maybe you already know
What I mean.
The water is warm.
We can watch the sun and then the moon, no demons to defeat.
The norm is freedom.
Keeping your thoughts
And not putting them back into
Your own remorse.
The drinks are free.
If they cost anything, they would be worth it.
Thinking with spirit with the one
Whom you want to be with
On the rainy days would be worth it.
Just be who you are and sit.
The clouds come in
Or leave, which is perfect.
And when you leave the sand and say
That it was a nice day,
Knowing in this world,
When we temporarily walk away
From the sand,
From the beach,
Rain in my mind with our loved ones
In our hearts, which nobody can defeat.

Past Purgatory

I've been so many places,
But something's still just ain't fair.
A thought, a whisper,
A real hug and kiss hello and goodbye.
I have changed my ways, too, when left alone.
My worries start to pry.
How many times
Have I failed?
The words I have said
All without bail.
No more keys.
Over the years, left none.
Lies I pray to the sky
Pray for no more.
Keep away from me.
Lies don't want to set me free.
No one hears or sees.
It's hard to believe
Laughter is the best medicine.
But lies hurt, self just be.
I can only figure out
My own honesty
Because I'm living past purgatory.

A Short Goodbye

If I ever messed up
So badly, madly in love
With the fall sky,
Awaiting your reply.
So many
Passing by,
Neither looking for an answer
Or a question to deny.
A blessing, I want to fly away
To visit all the worldly things.
Make the best of the day
And what it brings.
God bless everything
To all, to you.
Who's the devil's advocate?
Through this life we must remain true.

Sound Theory

This is what I think about sound and music.
This is what I think about the history of
The big bang and comets.
Then swirls of stars and comets.
The sounds that started the earth's
Audiophonics.
There were also
Underground tectonics,
Volcanoes and explosions from comets.
And lava flows,
When heated and cooled,
There were vapor elements and smoke.
In millions of years, it made storms,
Lightning, and thunder.
Made the oceans, atmosphere,
And life under
Splashes from tidal water.
Life's first phase.
Larger life came on land.
And the sun's rays
Made radio and gamma rays.
Photosynthesis grew plants
That gave animals the oxygen they crave.
Carnivores made roars.
Sounds from species
We never saw before.
Darwin said

That we came from apes,
And dinosaurs were related
To the birds of this age.
We became the top of the food chain
And became chanting and bones.
I believe drums were the first instrument
On a song.
Primitive melodies
Became longer.
Maybe whistling, group clapping
Became less abstract,
Conclusive and stronger.
Civilizations with language and speech
Caused it to evolve.
Rituals, gatherings, battle drums.
Villages involved, chants learned,
Humans became more civilized.
Used wind and strings.
Experimented for centuries
To make different sound bearings.
Tones were made in an octave-free.
Instruments
Were all about notes and degrees:
Flats, sharps, chords.
Gospel,
Classical music of heaven.
What was felt and going on is what was heard
From the world out into the universe.
It still has not changed
To this day.

Sometimes when a culture doesn't understand
Another's song, it gets anxious, and
Today, the way of life
In sound and music
Is how you play
And how you use it.
Thinking of all these things
Is magic in the universe.
If you disagree with me,
Listen to your favorite song first.

Worldly Waters

I feel the world turning.
I see the clouds moving.
I see the tides coming.
I smell the world absolutely.
I taste life beautifully.
I feel the desert's feet.
The mind flowing answers.
The question is peace.
The great minds of the East and West,
The flavors of the feast.
Kings and queens live,
And all a people are we.
Princes' and princesses' births
Bring mothers and fathers to their knees,
Increase faith and hope for answers.
Be humble, and pray at least.
Sometimes quiet are the storms.
So are the stars,
Time and space,
Near and far.
Eternity, what is it?
Just meditate, if you like, about the power.
Seven stars, seven movements.
Ashes and flowers,
Polaris to the north,
Cities of great towers.
Heaven and earth,

Worldly water showers.
Everything up and underneath,
For now and up above.
Wicked are these pickets.
Green we build it up.
Put away fire.
It's all about love.

Lightning Source UK Ltd.
Milton Keynes UK
UKHW041043070220
358341UK00003B/95

9 781532 092312